# MAKING MONEY
## IN
## STOCK TRADING

# MAKING MONEY

## IN

# STOCK TRADING

**BARRON'S**

*National Business and Financial Weekly*

NEW YORK, N. Y.

# FOREWORD

This book represents a series of articles published first in Barron's that was written originally in the form of letters to his sons by a business man who has successfully traded in securities as a side-line for some twenty years. Written from a frankly speculative point of view, these letters maintain that some people are "cut out" for making money by buying and selling stocks, while others are not. The only way to find out, the writer believes, is to try, but to be willing to admit failure if a few years' test does not bring favorable results.

The line between speculating and investing, however, is a thin one at best, and much of the practical advice which the author of this series is passing along to "the younger generation" may interest people who think of themselves only as "investors," as well as those who share the author's speculative viewpoint on the stock market.

The writer of these letters wishes to remain anonymous.

# CONTENTS

# 1

## The Stock Market as A Spare Time Job

WHEN ADVICE is being passed out to the next generation, it is the fashion, I believe, to classify the stock market along with wine, women and song. Passing the question as to whether this classification is fair to wine, women and/or song, it may be observed that although not so attractive as the other three, the market has certain advantages in that it can be distinctly more profitable and is subject to being understood without so much independent research.

As a steady provider it is hopelessly unreliable but, for a person who happens to be cut out for the work, it should be a very satisfactory spare time job. Since one is foolish to ignore any easy money which may be lying about, I am going to try to tell you what twenty years have, or at least should have, taught me, and encourage you to try your hand at it. By easy money, I don't mean that you will not have to work hard mentally or that you will be entirely free from acute distress of the vanity or pocket-book, but it is easy in the sense that the hours are short—perhaps two a week—and it can all be done from a comfortable chair.

The statement is frequently made that eighty or ninety per cent of the people who play the market lose money. This can be true only if there are included the many people who buy a stock in the same spirit in which they would put a stack of chips on number seven. If a gambler confined himself to well known stocks, making his selections from these by lot, and tossed a coin to decide whether to buy or sell, he should come out about even with commissions representing the house's only percentage against him. Since, however, the wide swings in which most stocks participate are the result of definite reasons and not pure chance, it should be possible to learn enough about the reasons to give the player the small advantage necessary for success. If you are right eight times out of fifteen, it will be worth the trouble. In fact, you do not even have to be right that often if you have any success at all in the speculator's constant endeavor to cut losses short and let profits run.  In looking over my records for the past twenty years, I was astonished to find that I had dealt in the securities of over three hundred different companies—far too many—making several trades in a number of them and that while the net results have been not unfavorable the number of losing trades actually exceeded by a small margin the number of winners.

These letters are not going to provide you with a system for hitting the jack-pot.  Your success, if any, will depend on your own knowledge, intelligence and character—my aim being to supply you, if possible, with an easier way of gaining some of the knowledge than acquiring it through losses.  There is little, if any, originality in what I have written; in fact, in all probability, even parts I might think are original have been said or written many times.  However, the ideas are all collected in one place, the collection is the result of much sifting and, unless otherwise stated, the conclusions are based not on theory but on actual experience, which means my mistakes.

After reading these letters, it may occur to you that since I have reached so many conclusions, I must have made a great many mistakes and therefore can't be very good at the job.  This deduction is unassailable and it furnishes the whole point of these letters.  If I thought one had to have exceptional ability to make money in the market, I wouldn't suggest that you try it.

In order to make a fair test you will have to risk some losses.  Paper trading won't do, as you can never tell thereby how you will act when you have real money on the line.  However, you don't have to plunge—a few years of trading in ten or twenty-share lots should give you your answer and not cost you more than two or three thousand dollars at the most.  If you find you are not a success, I would urge you to turn your money over to the best investment adviser you can find, tell him that your sole interest lies in preserving your principal, and never look at a stock quotation again.

# 2

## The Starting Point of Speculation

THE MOST difficult and at the same time the most important part of stock speculation is to decide whether the market as a whole is going up or going down or, if it is exhibiting no decisive trend, whether the next move will be up or down. If you can't make up your mind on this point, then stay out of the market. No matter how brilliant you may be in selecting good stocks, it isn't going to do you any good if you buy them in a bear market because, with rare exceptions, all stocks go down in such a market. The good ones may go down less, but it is not much satisfaction to know that you have lost less money than you might have. Action in a bull market is not so uniform as in a bear market, but the vast majority of stocks rise in varying degrees.

There are two general ways of predicting the way the market as a whole is going: By attempting to predict the trend of business through business statistics and by the action of the market itself.

Every index of general business activity is an average of a number of factors, such as freight car loadings, electric power production, cotton mill activity, etc. Such a business index is obviously a record of what has happened and, by the time such an index has moved substantially one way or the other, you will generally find that the stock market has moved at least as far in the same direction, and often further. To be of any use, therefore, the statistics must predict changes in the business index. The search for a reliable device of this nature has consumed as much time as the efforts to make gold out of baser metals, and has not been much more successful. This does not mean that you should totally ignore statistics of this nature, because if a group of such indexes all point in one direction their combined advice should, of course, be given serious consideration.

In one of these letters I will tell you about some types of indexes which appear to make more sense than others, and you should naturally be on the lookout for any new ones which may be developed, but I am in no position to emphasize the importance of this pursuit because in my own case whatever little success I have had in forecasting the future course of the market has come, not from any outside statistics, but from the action of the market itself.

You can look at an elevator and tell whether it is going up or down, and there are times when you can look at the stock market and tell just as easily; however, as a usual proposition, the market is a mass of cross-currents, some stocks apparently strong and others weak, but the market as a whole, as indicated by the averages, showing no conclusive trend that you can discern merely by watching it a while in a broker's office.

In the same way, if you just watch the ocean for five minutes you can't tell if the tide is coming in or going out, but if you wait until a big wave comes along and plant a stick on the shore at the highest point it reaches and then plant other sticks for succeeding waves, if the tide is coming in your last sticks will be higher up on the beach and if the tide is going out they will be lower. This is the essence of the so-called Dow theory about the stock market. It starts with the basis, which can be simply verified by looking over the market records of the past, that a trend in one direction, once started, usually continues over a long enough period of time and for a long enough distance to make it worth while following. By watching the successive waves as the market flows in and out to see if they are higher or lower, you will be able to see the way the tide is running and can follow it.

There is no method of predicting the market that is perfect, but this Dow theory is clearly one of the best. You should study it very carefully, and for this purpose should by all means read *The Stock Market Barometer*, by William Peter Hamilton and the *Story of the Averages* by Robert Rhea. It would also be well to read a collection of Robert Rhea's weekly letters on the Dow theory

---

*The Stock Market Barometer . . . . . . . . . . . . . . . . . . . . . . . $2.50
Story of the Averages . . . . . . . . . . . . . . . . . . . . . . . . . . . . $3.50
These books may be purchased from Barron's Book Dept., 30 Kilby St., Boston, Mass.

to see how he interpreted the market from week to week in the light of this theory.

Another valuable way of judging the market by its own action is to see how it reacts to news. To state the proposition briefly, if the market will not go down in response to bad news it is generally a buy, and if it will not go up in response to good news it is generally a sale. This theory works out better in predicting buying points than selling points, because at the top of a bull market stocks do not usually spend much time waiting around for you to see how they react to the news. When they stop going up, they start down and go fast.

The typical formation at the top of a long bull market is two peaks, the second one being slightly lower than the first, but at the bottom of a bear market there is frequently a long, fairly flat level during which the market is very inactive but refuses to go down in the face of continued poor earnings reports, reductions in dividends, unemployment, etc.

By emphasizing the action of the market rather than business statistics, let me again repeat that I do not mean you to close your eyes to the latter, and certainly do not mean that you should stop using your head in interpreting facts outside the market. For example, Scandinavia is one of our chief sources of supply for wood pulp, and when Germany invaded Norway it looked as if our imports of pulp would be cut off for the duration of the war, and, therefore, that pulp stocks might be a good buy. They enjoyed an agreeable rise and about a month later Germany attacked the Netherlands and was evidently aiming at France and Britain. In view of Germany's all-out method of Blitzkrieg war, it was reasonable to expect that Germany would either defeat France or be defeated herself within a fairly short period. What should one do, therefore, about the pulp stocks? It did not take much thought to produce the following conclusions:

(a) If Germany were defeated, the supplies of pulp from the Scandinavian countries would start coming in again which would be bad for pulp stocks,

(b) If France were defeated, the threat of our being involved in the war would have such a serious effect on our economic system that all stocks would be badly affected, and thus that no matter what was to happen pulp stocks should be sold immediately.

This is as good a place as any to emphasize the necessity of not letting your mind become paralyzed by events however much of a shock they may be.    Never forget to think.    Whenever something happens, start thinking how it will affect your stocks.    Try to put yourself in a detached frame of mind so that you are really thinking and not just worrying.    A good way of doing this is to look at your list of securities and say to yourself, "Suppose I didn't own any stocks and someone to whom I was under obligation came to me with this list and asked me what to do, what would I tell him?"    Keep on thinking until you come to a conclusion and then follow up the thinking with prompt and decisive action.

# 3

## Experience With the Dow Theory

ONE NEED NOT BUY EVERY TIME the Dow theory gives a buy signal, but it is to my mind absolutely essential to follow the rule of selling whenever the Dow theory gives a sell signal. To emphasize the point, I will trace the course of the averages over the past dozen years and, in passing, will mention certain temptations which led me away from obeying the above dictum.

The market had been going up steadily prior to 1928, each upward swing being higher than the preceding one, until the peak about the first of September, 1929. Then came a sharp drop in September followed by a rise in the early part of October. If the bull market were to continue, this rise should have carried the averages above the September peak, but, when the market started to fall without reaching this peak, the first sign of danger was given. The market might, however, before going lower than the bottom of the September reaction, have turned around and headed up again, which would have meant clear weather. According to the Dow theory, there is not a definite change in trend until the market not only fails to better the previous high point but also goes lower than the preceding reaction.

### The Warning by the Dow Theory

Toward the end of October, however, the market broke the bottom of the September reaction slightly on Wednesday, October 23, and with a vengeance on Thursday, October 24. The next day William Peter Hamilton, the author of the book previously mentioned, printed an editorial in *The Wall Street Journal*, entitled *A Turn in the Tide*, in which he stated that under the Dow theory the bull market was over and further trouble was ahead. I hadn't heard much of the Dow theory by then, but I started to read the editorial and it shocked me so that I didn't pay any attention to it. Things had gone on so well for five years and I was so sure that American Telephone and Eastman Kodak and several other stocks I owned were headed for substantially higher prices that I couldn't force myself to realize that the party was over or even seriously contemplate such a possibility.

Another thing that tended to benumb my mind was that I had already lost quite a bit in Thursday's sharp break. You will find that nothing beclouds the mental processes more than a bad drop in the market when you own stocks. The market did not move much that Friday and Saturday, but Monday the knife was plunged in even deeper, and I finally got out at the opening on Tuesday morning. Inside of two weeks the market was substantially lower than the point at which I sold, but I had obviously bungled things very badly. (You will hear more about stock market services later, but if you are ever tempted to depend upon them, you might keep in mind that two of the best, to which I was then subscribing, sent me wires on Friday stating that the Thursday reaction had completed the drop and that the market was then a buy.)

### History Repeated in 1937

You will notice in tracing the averages for the following three years that after the spring of 1930 there was no place at which an upward rally in both averages carried to a point higher than the preceding rally until the rise in the middle of 1932 which signaled the upward trend. From 1932 to 1937 there was no decline which went below the preceding decline until early in September, 1937, when the market dropped under the June low. My 1929 losses had made me tentatively decide that the next time there was a bear market signal under the Dow theory I would sell out. However, that was eight years before and things were going superbly in 1937. I had some stocks which I believed would unquestionably advance further so I indulged in a bit of thinking as to why the Dow theory would probably not work this time and brought up the following pretty good reasons:

(a) The break was due to a war scare and since war throws all rules out the window the Dow theory was not dependable under these circumstances.

(b) We were under a managed economy in which the Government could do about anything it wanted

with economics.   The President had recently con-
gratulated himself on the upward course of business
by telling reporters, "We planned it that way", and
I was beguiled by the thought that he would do something to stop a depression even if he had to print money.

(c) I read an economic letter by a very intelligent
man who said that for various reasons, particularly the
fact that we were going to have such good crops at such
high prices that fall, there could not be a serious depression, and

(d) The Dow theory had given false sell signals
before—it did in 1926—and was probably doing it again.

All these made up quite an attractive siren song,
to which I unfortunately listened with favor.

These two experiences made me finally determine—
with satisfying results in the spring of 1940—that I
would sell whenever the Dow theory gave a sell signal.
I think that if you ever take up stock trading you should
pin this rule on the wall and read it every day, if necessary,
so as to be sure that you will follow it.   Even if the signal
is a false one, there is nothing to stop you from getting
back in the market when the signal is later corrected by
the averages making new highs.   If there is one thing
about the market I am sure of, it is that following this rule
will save you over the years very much more money than
it will lose for you.   When the rule says sell, then sell
them at the market, sell them fast, and sell everything that
looks like a common stock.   Don't play favorites.   For
example, don't say to yourself, "While the market is
probably going down, such-and-such a stock is so obviously
cheap at these prices that it can't decline much, if any, and
I might be mistaken about the market's going down, so I
had better hold at least this stock."

I am sure that this is wrong and, if you will take
my word for it instead of learning by experience, you will
save yourself any quantity of both worry and money.
In case you need a little convincing, all you have to do is
look over the records of the past bear markets and see
what happened to the best stocks.

### Bear Markets Bring Changed Standards

One reason that it is wrong to save your pet stock

is that in a bear market the things that make the stock look cheap disappear and, on top of that, standards of value change.  For instance, if you have a stock that is only selling at twelve times earnings as against a standard of eighteen times earnings for most stocks in the same industry, you may have a very good thing.  But when a bear market in stocks and business comes along, not only your stock's earnings decline, but the standard of eighteen times earnings will also collapse, so that the stock will decline a great deal more than its earnings decline.  When business deteriorates, earnings that you think are impregnable disappear quickly and standards that you have been relying on go twice as fast.  If there is such a thing as a normal ratio of price to earnings for a stock, then in a bull market when investors have confidence that the earnings of a particular stock are on the increase, it will sell somewhat higher than the normal ratio, while in a bear market when they are afraid earnings will decrease, the stock will sell under the normal ratio. The net result is that the stock drops much farther than the decline in its earnings appears to warrant.

There are other phases of the Dow theory which you will learn by reading the books, and there are other mechanical ways of forecasting the stock market, such as lines, triangles, moving average trend indicators, etc. I believe you should read about them all just to know what they are, but I do not think any of these systems is reliable.

### Dow Theory Signals Late

You will notice that if you haven't bought or sold out sooner for other causes, following the Dow theory means that you will miss the tops and bottoms by quite a bit. This is one of the reasons that makes it so hard to follow. For example, in 1937, I had a stock that sold at about 80 in August and by the time the Dow theory sell signal came along it was a little under 60.  This seemed like a tremendous drop already and I couldn't bring myself not only to give up all the profits which I had hoped to make between 80 and 100 but also the profits which I had let slip through my fingers between 80 and 60, so I listened to that siren song I've told you about and didn't sell until a few months later when I read one of its monthly reports in an evening paper, which looked so bad that I put in a market order to sell the next morning and got 39. The stock eventually went to 22, so that was better than not selling at all, but failure to follow the Dow theory cost me some 15 or 20 points.

The temptation to keep your own stocks because of "special conditions" even though you think there is going to be a bear market is almost irresistible. For example, the best information I could procure in 1937 indicated that there was still a world-wide shortage of the product made by one of the companies in which I was interested and one of the arguments I used in persuading myself to keep this particular stock was that, in view of this world-wide shortage, the price of the product would at least hold up even if it did not advance, as was confidently expected, and that if the price of the product held up the earnings of the companies in this line of business were bound to continue at a very high rate. Moreover, my particular company had contracted to sell its output many months ahead. The information about the shortage and the probable trend of price came from the president of the company and I have no doubt that it was absolutely true. The trouble was that when the 1937 depression got into full swing, the demand for the product fell off abruptly, the contracts were canceled, the worldwide shortage disappeared, and there was, in fact, an over-supply which resulted in price cutting, and that ended the alleged "special condition."

In May, 1940, there was another Dow theory sell signal shortly following the German invasion of the Netherlands, and it would have been very easy to keep war stocks on the theory that now that the war was speeding up the demand for armament would increase. However, despite this "special condition", the war stocks dropped just as much, if not more than, the others.

Another kind of "special condition" results from wheedling yourself into the frame of mind that you are holding a stock like General Electric as an "investment" and are therefore not going to pay any attention to fluctuations. From 1930 to 1932, General Electric dropped to 10, from 90, with the result that your whole principal at the end of two years was worth only about two years of income on the price of 90.

## Buying for Income Fallacy

Another tempter is the notion that you are holding a stock for its dividend return and that you don't care what happens to the principal. You say to yourself "I am getting $6 a year from this stock now and I have no intention of selling it, so it doesn't make any difference what the price of the stock is as long as I keep it in the safe deposit box and get $6 a year." The trouble is that if a business depression comes along the company's earnings will be reduced and so will its dividend.

Still another reason for holding stocks is fear of the income tax you will have to pay next March 15th on the profit. I can assure you that this is a very successful way of avoiding income tax, not only for the next March 15th but forever—because your profit will disappear. It is a serious mistake to allow your judgment on cashing in profits to be influenced by taxes, and, incidentally, it is just about as ill-advised to sell a stock for the purpose of registering a tax loss (unless you replace it with one equally as good) as to avoid selling it for fear of the taxable gain. You cannot take a tax loss if you repurchase the stock within thirty days before or after the sale. If you want to stick to the same stock make your repurchase thirty-one days *before* the sale. If you wait until thirty-one days after the sale, four times out of five the stock will have gone up and you won't repurchase. This curious state of affairs is probably due to the fact that you only need a tax loss when you have gains to offset and the presence of gains usually signifies a bull market.

I could go on and name many more special conditions—almost every stock has a special condition—but I hope this is enough so that the first time you start thinking of a special reason for holding a stock after the sell signal has arrived, you will pick up the telephone and put in an order to sell before you can convince yourself.

If you do get caught and hold your stock through a panic in the market from which there is a fast rebound, sell out on the rebound. Before another bull market starts, stocks will almost invariably drift down to the panic lows if not lower.

# 4

## The Best Industries for Speculation

THERE ARE SOME INDUSTRIES which are always making progress and others which seem never to get anywhere or are addicted to treacherous behavior, and you might as well stick to the first type. Even though a stock in a poor industry looks like a bargain which "ought" to go up, it is better to buy something else and not argue. My current list of securities to avoid in peacetime—many of them are good during a war—includes oil, shipping, packaged foods, sugar, leather, rubber, silk, dairy, woolen, can manufacturing, luxury, "one gadget", and railroad stocks. You will have to make up your own list when the time comes and change it frequently because the conditions which make stocks good or bad investments are constantly changing.

### *Industries that Do Not Qualify*

However, as a suggestion of the qualities to look for, here is a brief and superficial outline of the reasons for my list:

#### OIL

Demand is increasing, but available supply and underground storage (i. e., shut-in wells) have always exceeded demand. The war may change this, but in the past there has been more chance of losing money and patience in these stocks than of making anything from them.

#### SHIPPING

Dependent on government subsidy. Bad labor conditions.

#### PACKAGED FOODS

No recent growth. Subject to competition from private brands of chain stores.

#### SUGAR

Any farming business with supply subject to nature's whims is bad. Price subject to political control through tariffs.

#### SILK, WOOL AND LEATHER

Declining industries by reason of substitutes, e. g., rayon, nylon, fabrikoid, etc.

#### RUBBER

Constantly recurring inventory troubles. Raw material subject to political control of foreign nations. Chaotic retail situation in tires.

### DAIRY
Squeezed between the farmer and the baby. Great competition and constant political meddling.

### CAN MANUFACTURING
No signs of recent growth, probably due to various factors such as increased popularity of frozen foods, use of other materials for containers, etc.

### LUXURY
The perfume and beauty cream business are obviously subject to whims which men have been unable to control for centuries.

### ONE GADGET
When a company makes only one gadget, like a coupler for railroad cars or a horn for automobiles, you will never know that its contracts have been canceled or that someone has invented a better gadget until the stock has dropped to nothing.

### RAILROAD
Still losing traffic to trucks and airplanes.

The necessity of making frequent changes in such a list is well illustrated by rubber stocks. If synthetic rubber proves as satisfactory as it is said to be, these companies will have a dependable supply of raw material at stable prices.

## *Three Desirable Groups*

Of the remaining stocks, there are three general types:

A—Companies which are constantly growing through new inventions, new uses, or wider demand, such as chemicals, certain types of machinery and equipment, and electric power;

B—Consumer industries which have fairly steady earnings and whose stocks therefore do not swing around so much. The best example is the tobacco stocks. Others are soft drink stocks and chain grocery store stocks;

C—The so-called heavy industry stocks, which have the widest swings and therefore make some of the best speculations. The typical example is steel, which is known as the prince or pauper industry. These swings are the natural result of the fact that people continue to smoke cigarettes, eat food, etc., at almost the same rate in bad times as in good times, but in bad times there is much less building, railroad construction, automobile production, etc., all of which require steel.

The one most important factor in any speculation is the probability of increased earnings, and from this point of view many of the best types of stock are found in Group A, although there are stocks in Group B which, through vigorous management and development of new products, are just as desirable as many of those in Group A.

# 5

## What About Diversification?

DIVERSIFICATION IN INVESTMENT is of several types, such as diversification as to industry, i. e., buying stocks in a number of different industries; geographical diversification, i. e., investing in companies in different parts of the country; and diversification as to type of security, i. e., some bonds and some stocks, etc. Obviously, diversification tends toward spreading the risk and provides not only insurance against mistakes but also a better chance of picking a winner. As opposed to the diversification-adherents, there is another school of thought that says to put all your eggs in one basket and watch that basket. I am going to indulge in the platitudinous recommendation that you compromise between the two.

Diversification as practiced by many investment companies and investment counsellors seems to me completely fanciful. They start out by deciding that a man should have, say, 10% of his investments in chemicals, 8% in utilities, 4% in steels, etc., and go through practically every industry you can think of until they reach 100%. Where they divine these percentages I haven't the faintest idea, but they tell you that they vary the percentages in accordance with the outlook for the particular industry. It thus seems to me that they admit that they are putting part of your money in industries with a second-grade outlook. If the outlook for the chemical industry is twice as good as the outlook for the railroad industry, wouldn't it be better to take the money they would put in railroad stocks and buy more chemicals?

In addition to this process of diversifying investments by industries, they then take each of the industry percentages and split them up between different companies and will suggest, for example, that out of the allotment for steels you should have 15% in United States Steel, 25% in Bethlehem Steel, 5% in Youngstown, etc. If the outlook for all the steel companies is equally good so far as one can tell, it is clearly a good idea to purchase equal amounts of several companies because you thereby obviate the possibility of having all your funds in the one stock that acts badly. On the other hand, I suspect that very often they split up the money invested in the steel industry in such a way as to invest part of it in companies that they think are definitely inferior to others.

Regarding the one-basket school of thought, I think it may be the best theoretically, provided you actually could do a thorough job of watching the basket. The trouble is that you are so far away from the doings of Bethlehem Steel, du Pont, etc., that you really can't watch them in the sense of knowing just what they are doing every day. Since you can't really watch the basket, it seems to me that you are taking too big a risk by betting on any one with everything you have.

From my own experience, I would say that ten stocks should be an absolute limit, and perhaps six or seven would be better. If you already own ten different stocks and another good one comes along that you feel you must buy, pick out the one you own that you think is the poorest and sell it. If you are spread all over the board, as the saying goes, you are bound to be in inferior stocks without realizing it, you will find it too difficult to give them the attention they deserve, and you will be handicapped if quick decisions become necessary.

# 6

## Buy Things You Can Sell

ONE OF THE GREAT advantages of investment or speculation in stocks as compared to real estate or mortgages is that when you think you have made a mistake you can cash in at a minute's notice. An equal advantage is that you have a constant test of the wisdom of your investment. The quotations on the market are always there to show you whether you have been right or wrong, while if you buy a piece of real estate you may have made a great mistake and not know anything about it until you wake up five years later when you want to sell and find no buyers within 50% of your purchase price.

These advantages are so enormous that it is clearly an error to give them up, which you can very easily do by investing in the wrong kind of stocks. For example, if you buy a stock that is not listed on a stock exchange, you never know what it is selling for except when you inquire from your broker; and then if you decide you have made a mistake, you may spend a week trying to find a buyer and have to pay a large commission or profit to the dealer who does find the buyer for you.

Moreover, mere listing on a stock exchange doesn't guarantee an active market. For instance, I own a stock which though listed on one of the smaller exchanges, has not been traded in for a month. An inactive stock like this often looks extraordinarily attractive, and one reason it is cheap is just because it is so inactive and is therefore less desirable. You will not find so much trouble in buying these stocks, but when it comes to selling them it is often almost impossible. The only time you can make a satisfactory sale of such a stock is when the company's business is booming and the market is going up and that is the time that you always think it is going higher and so fail to sell. No one can expect to pick the top of a bull market, and if you place your selling orders after the market has turned down, you can generally sell United States Steel, American Telephone, etc., within at least a point or so of the latest quoted market price; but if you own an inactive stock, you will find that it has broken wide open, that there is no demand for it at all, and that when you sell you must do so many points below the last quotation.

A vicious feature of such a stock is that its unmarketability furnishes another argument not to sell even after you think a bear market is upon you. You say to yourself, "Well, I'm locked in and can't sell, so I'll just ride it through. The last sale was 48, my stock is already down from 65, and if I try to sell, I'd be lucky to get 40." This may be perfectly true, but if you do buy stocks like this, don't let the argument tempt you into not selling.

The net result is that I think it might be better if one stuck entirely to very active listed stocks but, since I don't believe you will follow this advice, as I don't myself, you ought to make a definite rule for yourself about the percentage of your funds you will have in inactive securities. You might fix, say, 30% as the limit and if you are already up to your limit and another good one comes along, sell out enough of those you have so that you keep within this limit.

# 7

## Which Stocks to Buy—And How to Buy Them

AFTER YOU HAVE DECIDED what industries you are willing to go into and which ones you want to stay out of, comes the problem of finding which stocks to select. There are two different solutions. One is to buy only the recognized leaders and another is to look around and try to find companies which you think are coming up and whose stocks may give you a greater than average profit. The second plan is more interesting and can produce greater than average profits, but is obviously susceptible of producing greater than average losses. Regardless, however, of which plan you follow there are certain things that you ought to do:

1—Find a stock whose earnings are on the increase. Always remember that the most vital thing in all stock speculation is to buy into a company whose earnings are probably going to be higher than they have been. Consequently, you should do everything you can to secure as much information as possible on present and prospective earnings. You may be able to secure this information through your broker or an investment adviser or some friend who knows someone in the company, etc.[1]

### *See If Your Stock Is Out of Line*

2—Compare your stock's recent market action with the recent market action of an average of a group of stocks in the same industry. Such a comparison is best made by means of charts. Unless your stock is at least as strong, if not stronger, than the average, there is something wrong with it.

3—Determine as best you can from the chart whether your stock is in an upward or downward trend. Do not be afraid to buy it just because it is selling higher than it

---

[1]—You might also subscribe to a good weekly financial publication.—Ed.

ever has before—this may well mean that it has finally hit its stride and is going much higher still—but try not to buy a stock that has been higher and looks as if it is on the way down. Stocks move in zigzags, and if a stock has had a long rise and its last top is lower than the preceding one, and if its last bottom is lower than its preceding bottom, it may well be starting a downtrend.

4—Do whatever you can to check on the ability and integrity of the management. It is often impossible to do more than look at the company's past record.

5—Examine the company's balance sheet to be sure that it has a strong enough financial condition so that it will live (this is a good deal more important in bad times than good) and look into its capitalization to see that it will have no trouble in handling maturing bonds and that its earnings are not artificially stated by a heavy capitalization of senior securities (more on this later.)

6—Compare its price-earnings ratio (i. e., market price divided by earnings per share) to the price-earnings ratios of other companies in the same line of business. Since present and prospective earnings are the most important factor in determining the market price of a stock, a relatively low price-earnings ratio is obviously desirable, but in and of itself it means little so far as speculation is concerned unless there is the probability of increased earnings in the future or the earnings are not generally known. If you learn that a company's earnings have increased substantially since its last published report and the stock has not reflected the improvement, it may be a desirable purchase even though no further increase can be reasonably anticipated.

## The Time to Get Out

However, you should sell a stock purchased under these circumstances shortly after the larger earnings are made public, even though the stock does not rise. You bought because you thought that the public would be eager to do likewise and would consequently put up the price as soon as it found out about the earnings. If the public does not behave in accordance with your plans for it, you have made a mistake in judgment which can be corrected only by selling. When your fundamental reason for entering into a transaction is the advantage you have from private information, you should close out the transaction as soon as you lose the advantage  One of the half-truths of Wall Street is applicable here, i. e., "Sell when the good news is out."

7—Determine, if possible, whether the earnings are over or under-stated.  For example, two chemical companies of equal desirability might report entirely different earnings if one charged research expenditures against earnings and the other capitalized them.  Again, two power companies of equal desirability might report entirely different earnings if one charged a higher rate of depreciation than another.

8—Try to secure an analysis of the stock prepared by a financial publication, brokerage house or investment service.  Such an analysis may frequently point out good or bad points which you have overlooked.

### Book Value as a Guide

9—Compare the book value (which is supposed to be cost of assets less depreciation and liabilities) of the company to the aggregate market value of its securities.  This comparison will be helpful if there is an excess profits tax in your day limiting earnings to a percentage of invested capital, and will also sometimes serve as a rough check on the price you are paying.

Book value is not, as a rule, a very significant factor in stock speculation except for its use as a guide at the top of a boom or the bottom of a depression.  For example, in 1932 many a good stock—Montgomery Ward is one that comes to mind—was selling so low that the company could have used its cash and other current assets to pay off all its debts, thrown away its plants and equipment, and still have had enough on hand to distribute to stockholders substantially more than the market price of the stock.  Situations of this kind only develop in periods of extreme depression and pessimism, but in such times your courage needs a little backing up and you will find it very helpful to realize that you are buying $10 bills for fives and getting the plant thrown in free.

### *Appraising Goodwill*

An example at the other end of the scale was furnished in 1933 by the stocks of liquor companies and companies which had plants equipped to make alcohol or planned to go into the liquor business on the repeal of prohibition, such as Standard Brands and Commercial Solvents. Out of the enormous rise in the aggregate market value of Commercial Solvents, I estimate that at least $40 million of the increase was due to liquor *prospects* alone, which were, of course, not represented by any tangible assets.

It was fairly obvious that the idea of going into the liquor business, which was not very original and was a free idea open to anyone, could not possibly be worth $40 million. Even if one could compile an estimate of profits which appeared to justify such a valuation, the inevitable consequence would be to attract so many into the business that the resulting competition might turn paper profits into actual losses. So when you find a company with $10 million of tangible assets and a market valuation of $50 million, ask yourself some questions, such as, "Is the goodwill of this company worth $40 million?" "Can the management make assets that cost $10 million produce an attractive return not only on their cost but also on another $40 million plus an additional amount which would make the stock a good buy?" The answer may be in the affirmative—it always has been for a company like Coca-Cola,—but there are not many others like it.

# 8

## Buy or Sell "At the Market"

THERE ARE TWO WAYS of placing orders, i. e., an order to buy or sell at a given price or an order to buy or sell "at the market", which means at the best price obtainable at the moment. If you give an order to sell at a specific price, sometimes you can get that price right away and other times you will have to wait for several days before the stock can be sold at that price and sometimes it can never be sold.

Buying and selling at specific prices is very intriguing. You will say to yourself that stocks are always fluctuating up and down a little bit and it is silly for me not to get the top of one of those fluctuations when I sell and the bottom when I buy. If I put in an order to sell at market. my broker will have to go on the floor and make the best deal he can right away, which probably won't be as advantageous as fixing a reasonable price and waiting for the other party to meet it.

### Don't Put a Limit on the Price

This is absolutely the wrong way to do business. If you think a stock is going down, the only way to sell it is to sell it fast and sell it at the market. If you follow this advice, there will be many times when you will get, say, 58 for your stock and find that it closed that day at $58\frac{1}{2}$ or more and you will regret that you didn't save the difference by putting in a limit order, but I can assure that this regret won't be anywhere near so poignant as the regret to which you will be subject if you follow the limited-order theory of doing business and occasionally find that your stock is down ten points without ever having touched your limit. By following the limited-order theory of doing business, you chisel little savings here and there, but subject yourself to the possibility of enormous losses. Foregoing these little profits provides a cheap insurance premium. They aren't lost any more than insurance premiums are lost when you don't have a fire.

In the same way, if you have bought a stock and come
to think you have made a mistake, don't put in a limit
order which will get you out even and hope to sell at that
price; sell it at the market and take your loss.

This advice is simple enough to follow with active
stocks, but you may find yourself tempted to make exceptions with inactive stocks. However, there is no doubt
in my mind that you have just got to make yourself sell
out inactive stocks at the market wherever you can even
if your broker tells you that to do so would slaughter the
price. If you aren't willing to have the price slaughtered
when you come to sell the stock, don't buy it in the first
place. The "wherever you can" in the second sentence
above covers the case where there is no buyer at all. A
while ago I owned an unlisted stock which had practically
no market. The last sale I knew about was 17 and I told
the broker to try to find a buyer around 16, but to take
any reasonable offer. After a day or so I telephoned him
and asked him if he thought he could get 14 for it and he
replied that he could get 16 just as easily as 14, the only
question being to find someone to buy it at all. If you
think to yourself that the mistake I made in regard to this
stock was buying it at all, you will be right.

## The Same Applies to Buy Orders

The same general principle of dealing at the market
applies to purchases as well as to sales. It isn't quite so
important because stocks do not go up quite as fast or as
suddenly as they drop. Also, if you do not own a stock,
you lose nothing by not buying it, you just fail to have
a chance at a profit; while if you own it already, you may
very well lose a great deal by not selling it the right way.
However, even though not so important in the case of
buying, there is still no question in my mind that buying
"at the market" is the right way to do business. You will
lose much more by trying to save a point or so than you will
by stepping in and paying whatever you must. If you
don't buy at the market, here is the kind of thing you may
get into. You will decide to buy a stock which is selling
at, say, 21, and in looking over what it has been selling for
recently you notice that just yesterday it sold as low as $19\frac{1}{2}$.
You say to yourself, "It will surely have some little reaction
from 21," and so you put in an order to buy at $20\frac{1}{2}$, since

you are afraid if you put in a market order to buy you may pay 21¼, which is very likely.

Well, the stock doesn't go down to 20½ and in a day or so it is selling at 21¾. You will then say to yourself, "I could have bought it around 21¼ if I'd put in a market order, and I don't want to pay more than that," so you will raise your order to 21¼. The next thing you know the stock is 23 and you keep chasing it up, always lagging a point or so in your bid behind the market price, with the result that you either make no purchase at all or pay several points more than you would have paid if you had put in an immediate market order.

### *Some Brokers Try "To Do Better"*

You will have to fight your broker on this advice, because brokers make their profit on fractions of a point and, consequently, their mental attitude on the business is such that many of them think you are a bungler or mildly crazy if you put in a market order and buy a stock at 21½ when the last sale was 21, particularly when the broker thinks that by waiting around for several hours you ought to be able to pick it up at 21.

# 9

## Big Profits and Small Losses

WHEN YOU READ THIS HEADING, you may say to yourself, "Why that is a very lovely idea, but it is so obviously desirable that I hardly think any advice is necessary on the subject." The trouble is that you have to be very careful to avoid getting in a frame of mind in which you do just the reverse, and the purpose of this letter is to warn you about the pitfalls.

In the first place, you must never under any circumstances acquire the habit of buying for a quick turn and jumping in and out of the market. Some people may be good at it, although I've never met one who could make a profit and pay commissions. Commissions are about a quarter of a point and the difference between buying and selling prices on even an active stock is perhaps another quarter of a point, so that for a completed trade you have about a point of expense against you. If you are buying for a gain of ten points or more, this percentage against you is reduced to 10% or less, but on a two or three point profit the percentage is so high that you can't possibly be right enough times to pay the overhead and the losses. Moreover, even disregarding commissions. it is more difficult to predict minor fluctuations than major trends. Thus it is close to impossible for anyone to make a profit from quick turns, but it is *absolutely impossible* for anyone to do it as a side line to his regular business. There is practically a 100% chance of your being cleaned out if you do it long enough, and the necessary time and worry will completely unfit you for steady work.

### Long Profits—or Do Nothing

To simplify the matter, I make myself a rule not to buy anything unless I am prepared to hold it for six months or a year and there is a reasonable prospect of making at least a 50% profit in this time. If your attention is called to a stock selling for 30 that you think should go to 35 but you do not see any reasonable prospect of its going higher, don't fool with it.  It isn't worth the risk that you are wrong and the expenses, plus tying up your capital.

Once you have bought a stock and it starts up, be patient and let it ride.  Don't set any arbitrary limit of 50% (that is merely a test as to whether you are going to buy it or not), but stay with your stock as a general rule until you think its earnings are not going to continue growing, or you think a bear market has started.

The only exceptions are:

(a) Stocks you have bought on advance information or in anticipation of some particular development, and which you plan to "sell on the good news," and

(b) Stocks with a thin market which should generally be sold when you still think they are going higher because it is so hard to sell them later.  If they do go higher, it will console you to realize it is an absolute certainty that at least 90% of the stockholders will still be there long after the stock has dropped below your selling price.

There is a saying in the business, "You will never go broke taking a profit", the point being a sort of encouragement to sell whenever you have a profit.  The saying would contain more truth if they added the words "but you will never make any money either."  As it stands, it is either stupid or a swindle devised by brokers who are naturally interested in having you sell one stock to buy another.  A famous stock speculator once said he had made more money out of his patience in sitting with a good stock than his intelligence in buying it.

In order to sit with stocks, you must have peace of mind which means among other things that you must have not less than a 50% margin on active stocks and a 75% margin on inactive stocks and probably more as the market goes higher.  A bull market is not just a one way ride—there are frequent sharp and unpredictable breaks and if you are up to your limit on margin, you may be forced out at the bottom of one of these breaks.

However, with a satisfactory margin do not let the possibility of these breaks worry you.  When a broker tells you that the market looks overbought or that a reaction is overdue, or that a well-known stock market service is advising immediate sale of stocks, pay no atten-

tion to him.  In the first place the chances are a great deal
better than even that he is wrong or that the reaction will
be so small that you can't profit from it, and in the second
place even if you could know positively that he is right,
you should not sell unless you think the bull market is over
because you will lose your position and may never regain
it.  For example, assume that you have bought Case at
65 thinking it will go over 100 in a reasonable time,
that when it reaches 77 you decide it will react, that
you sell, and lastly that you were right about the reaction
and the stock starts dropping.  When do you repurchase?
At 75?  At 73?  At 71?  You won't know and neither will
anyone else because there is no basis for judgment on such
a matter.  If the stock has a fast rally above 77 while
you are worrying about what to do (which will happen
at least half the time)  you will start hoping for another
reaction and will not be able to bring yourself to buy back
at 80 and thus prove conclusively what a fool you have
been.   And if you do repurchase somewhere below 77,
you will have risked losing all the profit from 77 up for a
sheer gamble at a few points.

## Limit Your Losses

While you should be very slow to take profits, you
should be very quick to take losses.  If you buy a stock
at 50 and it goes to 45, you have made a mistake in buying
it, or it wouldn't have dropped so much. That is not to
say that stocks don't sometimes drop five or 10 points, or
even more, below your purchase price and then go up and
show a handsome profit in the end, but you will find that
this is rarely the case.  The fact that you made a mistake
in buying the stock at 50 should be an immediate red flag
to you because a mistake might very well, and often does,
turn out to be a fundamental one.  A drop of five or six
points after you buy a stock more often than not indi-
cates that there is something wrong with the purchase.
Some people adopt the rule of selling out any stock that
drops as much as 10% after they buy it.  I am not ready
to recommend that you blindly follow such a rule, but can
at least say that you would be doing very much better to
follow this kind of rule than to hold anything you buy. Be
very quick to recognize your mistakes and get rid of them.

## Keep the Good Ones and Sell the Poorest

I know a man who inherited a good deal of money and who does no work at all except looking after the investment of his inheritance. He keeps his money invested in twelve different common stocks and once a month religiously sells out the one that is doing the poorest. Here, again, you could probably do better than following such an arbitrary practice, but it is certainly much better than not following any practice at all in getting rid of your mistakes.

There is a modification of this plan, however, which I thoroughly recommend your following, and that is to go over your list at fixed times twice a year and sell at least one stock, unless you are fortunate enough to find that they are all selling above your purchase price and have gone up since your last examination. If, after you have sold your worst stock, you really think there is no better stock on the board which you don't already own, then buy it back again; but it is at least a ten to one bet that when you have gotten rid of it and given some thought to the matter you will discover other stocks you'd much rather have. This is a very good way of cleaning out your account of deadwood. If you don't do it, you'll find yourself getting married to stocks with a margin call the only ground for divorce.

Another excellent procedure to follow with all stocks which are not doing well is to ask yourself the question, "If I had the equivalent amount in cash, would I buy this particular stock or some other, or would I keep the cash?" There isn't the slightest compulsion on you to own common stocks, so that if the answer to your theoretical question is an inclination toward cash, you should sell immediately.

I have said that a drop in your stock of anything like 10% is a red flag. There are some circumstances in which it is not only a red flag but also an absolute command to sell, and that is when your stock drops and the rest of the market doesn't. If everything is going along as you expect it to go, you can be 90% sure of one thing and that is that if your stock behaves worse than the average of stocks of companies in the same line of business, or if the average of similar stocks behaves worse than the average of the market as a whole, there is something definitely wrong. The reports from the company may be very optimistic and you may not be able to see any possible reason why your stock is going down, but don't worry about reasons. Sell the stock and you'll find out the reasons later when the bad news comes out.

Every brokerage house has one or more statisticians or customers' men who keep charts of the market, and for very little money you could induce him to keep a chart of your stocks if he doesn't already do so. There are weekly publications which give the averages for a selected number of stocks in each group, such as oils, aircrafts, can manufacturing, etc., and at least once a week you should keep an eye on how your type of stock compares with the rest of the market and how your individual stock compares with others of its type.

There is an old saying in the market, which is one of the few good ones I know, and that is, "Don't argue with the tape." This means, don't be like the fellow who was behind bars, but insisted, "You can't put me in jail." Never think, "My stock simply can't go down in view of these wonderful earnings and prospects, etc." If your stock goes down and it shouldn't, your information is wrong.

Following this rule worked out well for me once in the spring of 1929, when I received what appeared to be very good information that Chrysler would earn something like $15 a share and should sell substantially higher. It was then selling at 118, so I bought quite a few shares. Everything went along all right for a day or so, and then suddenly the stock dropped to 114 on a day when the market as a whole was not weak. Fortunately, I had sense enough to do the right thing and sold my stock immediately. For all I knew Chrysler's business was booming, but it turned out that although the bull market had six months or more to run, the automobile business had already passed its peak and Chrysler was on its way to about 20 and never saw 114 again until seven or eight years later. When you say that a stock just can't drop in the light of certain supposed facts, you are making an absolutely true statement, so that since the stock *is* dropping you must conclude that the facts are wrong.

## *A Bitter Experience*

One very humiliating experience I had along these lines concerned the stock of a certain bank which I bought a number of years ago. The salesman who had induced me to buy also bought some for his own account. It looked very good and we were both thinking up ways of spending the forthcoming profits. One fine day it took a bad drop and continued to decline the next day. I telephoned the salesman and he promptly called to assure me everything was absolutely all right, that his firm had wired to head-quarters and that the bank was doing better than ever. I then delivered him a lecture about arguing with the tape and he had his office manager give me further assurances.

The net result, I regret to report, was that I held the stock. It kept on dropping for no apparent reason—you never know the reason until it is too late—and several months later it developed that certain officers of the bank had been guilty of dishonest practices, the bank went broke, and I was in for not only a total loss but possibly an assessment. Shortly thereafter I ran into the salesman on the street and asked him whether he was concerned about an assessment for his stock and he said to me, "That talk you gave me about arguing with the tape convinced me and I sold out my stock the next day."

## 10

## Averaging Down and Up

THE PRACTICE OF AVERAGING down can be illustrated as follows: You will select a desirable stock and buy some at, say, 50. It will then go to 45 and you buy some more, then to 40, and you buy still some more. You can see that the stock would have to recover to only 45 for you to be even again, while if you hadn't averaged down, it would have to come back to 50 before you would have been even. Here, again, is one of those ideas which looks superficially attractive and which I think is all wrong. As I see it, there are definite objections to this method of operating:

### *Doubling Up May Prove Disastrous*

1—It is something like betting on a color in a roulette game and doubling your bets each time you lose. Your color is bound to come up in time and if you keep on doubling your bets and there is no limit to the size of bet the house will take and no limit to your capital, you will ultimately win. However, if you follow this doubling scheme in practice, sooner or later you will run up against the limit and then the scheme completely breaks down. In the stock market your limit is your capital, which is dwindling rapidly if the stock is going down. I once averaged down neatly every two points from 30 to 18, where I ran out of money. The stock continued on to 10 and then came back to 20. If I had had enough capital to keep on buying every two points down to the bottom, I would have come out even when it came back to 20, but as it was my average price was about 24. Also, in addition to the limit of your capital, there is the limit of your nerve. There are plenty of stocks which never come back and if yours keeps on dropping and your capital is dwindling, there is some point at which you are going to get scared (perhaps wisely) and not buy any more even though you have the money, so instead of an average of the whole range of prices you may end up with an average of the high prices.

2—It may not work the same with you as with me, but it so happens that every time I tried averaging down, I was so relieved about recovering the loss when the stock came back to the break even point that I invariably sold and had all the worry and risk for nothing.

3—A more fundamental objection is brought out in the letter about taking your losses, i. e., when you have bought a stock that goes down you have made a mistake and most of the time there is less risk of loss and more chance of profit to be rid of your mistake and look around for a better opportunity than to stick to your mistake through thick and thin. When you do that you are acting more on hope and stubbornness than clear choice, and remember that while your color is bound to come up in time in a roulette game, your stock is not bound to come back.

In contrast to averaging down, there is a type of buying which might be called averaging up which is a very good way of buying a stock. For example, suppose you determine that a stock is a good buy at 30 and that you would like to buy 300 shares. You first buy 100 shares at the market, and we'll say the stock does nothing for a while but fluctuate back and forth between 29 and 31 If it should drop some day to 27, you would immediately think about selling it, but as long as it moves around within a small range of your purchase price you sit patiently and wait. Then, if some day the stock goes over 31, it looks like you have made a pretty good buy at 30 and you buy another 100 shares at the market. Then if the stock continues to act well and goes on up to 32 you buy your last 100 shares. In this way, as you make each purchase you already have a little profit and you have tested out the stock and found that it was acting well and that from all appearances your judgment was correct in buying it.

## Buying for the Rise

It is true that a reaction to 31 will wipe out your profit, while if you had bought all of the stock at 30 you would still have a profit, and if it were pure chance whether the stock were going up or down then it would probably be better to buy all of it at 30. But you are not

buying on the basis of pure chance; you are buying because your judgment tells you the stock will go up, and
the mere fact that the stock has gone up tends to confirm
your judgment and increases the chances that you were
right in the original purchase.  You will lose a part of your
potential profit in buying in this way, but remember that
you are not buying for a few points profit but for at least
a 50% profit and the amount that you lose is good insurance against the cases when you buy at 30 and a week later
the stock looks sick at 27.

# 11

## Profits Through Short Selling

WHEN YOU THINK A STOCK is going up, you buy it first and sell it later. When you think it is going down, you sell it first and buy it later. Since you must make actual delivery of anything you sell, if you sell a stock when you don't own it, i. e., sell it short, your broker will borrow the stock from somebody so you can make delivery to the buyer. Then when you buy it back, the broker uses the stock you have bought to repay the loan.

In the past it was possible for operators to drive a stock below what would otherwise be its market price by large short sales. This artificial lowering of prices has been criticized on the ground that it disturbed general confidence and thereby tended to hurt business. Under the present short selling rules, however, a stock cannot be sold short at less than the last preceding price, and, consequently, these drives in which stocks were sold at any price just to knock them down have been eliminated.

Even under the present short selling rules, however, you will no doubt find a number of people who criticize short selling either on the ground that it is pure gambling or that there is something anti-social about it in that even though it can no longer be used to drive the prices of stocks down, it at least may have the effect of keeping them from going as high as they otherwise would. Such criticism usually emanates from people who like to think they are investing when they buy common stocks, even though they are speculating or gambling just as much as you are if you sell them short, or from people who have an odd notion that there is something unpatriotic about doing your bit to prevent United States Steel from selling higher. Naturally, the most violent critics are those who have lost money through owning stocks while others have made money by selling them short.

## Uses of Short Selling

I think it is very important indeed for you to accustom yourself to short selling for two reasons:

1—You can make money much faster selling short than buying—if you are right—because stocks drop much faster than they go up.

2—A familiarity with short selling and a readiness to sell stock short is one of the greatest possible aids in keeping the profits you have made from buying stocks.

To illustrate this last point, you can look upon playing the market as a bridge game. Opportunities to sell short occur about one-fourth as often as opportunities to buy, just as opportunities of bidding no trump occur about one-fourth as often as opportunities of bidding one of the suits. Now suppose that you were playing bridge and for some reason were opposed to bidding no trump, but, nevertheless, liked the game very much. You can readily see that you would be tempted to stretch doubtful suit bids in order to stay in the game even though the proper bid was no trump.

In the same way, if you are playing the market and you find short selling very difficult to accustom yourself to and don't like to do it at all—but, nevertheless, like the game, i. e., like to make profits out of the market—you will tend to stretch and overemphasize the possibility of profit from buying just in order to keep in the game. If you have bought a stock at 50 and it is selling at 70 and you think it is going to 90, and then something happens which makes you think it would be safer to get out, you will find it psychologically much more difficult to sell if this means that you must give up the opportunity of profit. You will probably have thought how nice the profits will be when the stock gets to 90 and to divorce yourself from these profits entirely by selling is often too big a wrench. On the other hand, if you are accustomed to short selling and are ready to go into it whenever the time looks right, you won't mind so much because you will say to yourself that you don't care how you make the profit, you would just as soon make it when the stock goes down as up.

## Why Short Selling Is Difficult

You may wonder at the reason for all this emphasis on accustoming yourself to short selling and it may at first glance seem to you no more difficult to bring yourself to sell a stock short than to buy one. This is very far from the case. All you have to do is sell something like General Electric short and the following begins to happen to you:

(a) You think that when you buy a stock all it can do is go down to zero, while if you sell a stock short there is no limit to where it can go, and that you might lose everything you have from a sudden rise in this one stock alone. You can't get your mind off the possibility of a fight for control of the company which may drive the stock up way beyond what it is worth, or famous corners in the past like the Stutz corner, which sent Stutz Motor stock up some 300 points in a few weeks;

(b) You will read in the papers about a possible drive against the shorts or possible legislation to prohibit short selling, which would make all the shorts cover at once at great loss, and

(c) You will be unable to forget J. P. Morgan's alleged advice not to sell America short, and you will think to yourself that you are short one of the best stocks in the world, let alone the United States, and that not so long ago it sold 50 or 100 points higher and may be on its way back up.

The only way to accustom yourself to short selling is to start with a small enough number of shares so that you won't worry and gradually increase the dose. You should make up your mind now that if you ever speculate in stocks you will sell some stock short, even if it is only ten shares, the first time you think we are in a bear market.

## Short Sales as Hedges

Another possible advantage of short selling comes in using it as a hedge. Suppose you are long some stock with a very thin market and the market starts going down and you feel that you should get out, but that you are locked in and just can't sell your long stock; I still think, as stated in a previous letter, that the thing to do is to sell the stock for any price you can get for it, but if you can't bring yourself to adopt this course, you should at least sell short an equal number of shares of some active stock with a big capitalization.

As a general proposition, it is best not to do what is known as feeling for the top, i.e., making short sales hoping that the top has come. If you own a stock you think is too high, you may sometimes secure a better result by selling it than waiting for the turn, but don't go short at the same time, because the mere fact that a stock looks high is no reason that it won't go very much higher. In short selling, it is better to wait until you think the turn has come and then act very quickly.

Speed and decisiveness are essential to stock trading, and this is particularly true when it comes to any kind of selling. Stocks drop so fast once they have started that when you decide you should sell, do it immediately without horsing around. Mulling things over is all very well in other lines of pursuit, but it will ruin a trader in stocks. If you like to mull, do a lot of hypothetical mulling before the occasion arises. You can put questions to yourself like, "If war is declared, what will I do?" or, "I expect such-and-such a stock to earn $8 a share this year. If it reports only $7 a share, what will I do?" This practice of asking yourself questions will keep your reasoning powers in trim and make it easy for you to proceed without delay when the time comes.

# 12

## The Delusion of Income

ONE OF THE BIGGEST DELUSIONS in the world is to buy common stocks for income. There are many idiotic sayings about stocks, but my candidate for the number one position is the remark, "I buy stocks for income, so am not concerned about a market decline." There might be some sense to this idea if you could buy common stocks for income, but this is so obviously impossible that I can't see why anyone even thinks of it. There are a few outstanding exceptions, notably American Telephone. All you have to do to verify this statement is to look back over the dividend records of leading stocks for the past ten or fifteen years.

### No "Regular" Dividends

One striking example can be found in railroad stocks. I venture to say that in 1932 and again in 1938 at least 80% of the railroad stocks were selling for less than one year of dividends in 1929 and, of course, they weren't paying any dividends at all by the time they fell this low. A dividend return on a stock means nothing and calling it a "regular dividend" gives no additional assurance that it will persist. The only reason for ever inquiring about the dividend rate is to make sure it isn't too high. The minute a dividend return is higher than that obtainable from the average of stocks, you have an immediate warning that it may be cut, which is, in turn, a warning that the company is not doing so well. In fact, if dividend return were your sole guide, it would be better to buy the stocks that give you the lowest income rather than the ones that give you the highest.

### Income from Capital

Even if you happen to be convinced of the correctness of these ideas regarding dividends, you may say that you need some income from your speculative account and that therefore you are forced to cast an eye at the dividend rate in selecting your purchases. There is, however, a mechanical device which meets this objection and frees you completely from worrying about dividend returns. This device is to pay no attention to your dividends, but have your broker pay you an amount each month which represents a reasonable return on your equity. For example, if you have an equity of $30,000 in a brokerage account and the current rate of return on good public utility preferred stocks is 4%, you could expect to earn 4% on $30,000 if you took your funds out of the market. Accordingly, you instruct your broker to pay you $100 a month out of your account regardless of dividends received and, if your stocks are wisely selected, they will more than make up the $1,200 in a year even if they pay no dividends. Remember that on a stock selling at $25 a share, a 4% dividend is only one point a year and many stocks vary this much every day.

# 13

## Keeping Your Profits

THIS IS NOT A LETTER on how to invest your money, but on how to have some money to invest.

One of the chief dangers of being successful in the market is that you are likely to look upon the profits as chips in the game, and not as money. You acquire somewhat the same attitude as a group playing poker for $10 chips with the understanding that when the game is over they settle for 1% of the amounts owing. If a man works hard and saves money, or even if he inherits some money, he looks upon the capital as "real" money and tries to keep it, but $2,000 made on the market doesn't look anything like as big as $2,000 made from hard work.

### *Draw Down Half the Earnings*

Just a warning of this danger won't do you much good, but here is a mechanical device which, if followed religiously, will, I think, help you a great deal to keep what you make. The device is the very simple one of taking half your profits out of the market. In other words, suppose you make $3,000 on a transaction. You use it first to apply against any losses and then take half the balance out of your brokerage account and invest it in something which you put in your safe deposit box. Once in your safe deposit box, never under any circumstances take it out unless you wish to change it for something else to put back, except that if you have the misfortune to be practically cleaned out, then you can deliberately take some of the securities out of the safe deposit box and sell them and use the proceeds to start over again. In connection with this plan, here are a few warnings:

1—By *invest* the money, I mean put it into something that you don't expect will go up or down much, such as a bond or preferred stock or a few bank stocks. Don't allow yourself to be beguiled by sayings like, "A good investment is also a good speculation" or that, "The way to avoid losses is to keep making profits." Don't chisel on the plan by buying convertible securities unless you can see by direct comparison with other bonds or preferred stock that they are worth their price as securities without the conversion privilege, and don't fall for the idea that everyone should have a little General Electric and put some of your "investment" funds in stocks of that kind. All you want is a reasonably safe place for your money so that you can get it out when you want it and have it give you some return in the meantime. I don't mean that you have to stick to government bonds—the preferred stocks of most utility operating companies are good enough even though they may swing 20% above and below par.

2—Don't look upon the investment fund as a possible source from which to meet margin calls. If you receive a margin call, sell out enough stocks in your brokerage account to meet it. The only time you should ever put your investment money back in the market is after the excitement is all over and you have lost so much that you need more tools to work with and you deliberately take out some of the investment fund in order to make new commitments which you think will be profitable and not to protect old ones that have already proven to be mistakes.

3—If you are carrying stocks on margin, don't say to yourself, "The safest investment is to pay off my own debts, so I will have my speculative account borrow from my investment account so that my speculative account pays interest to my investment account instead of to the broker." This is all very well in theory, but in practice you will begin looking upon the money you have borrowed from your investment account as part of your speculative account.

It is very important to have your speculative account stand on its own feet and not become involved with your investment account or with other commitments. For example, if you have some income taxes to meet on your profits or you are planning to buy or build a house, take the money out of your speculative account and put it in the bank even if you are getting no interest from the bank and have to pay interest to the broker, and I don't mean by this take it out mentally—actually take it out and put it in the bank and forget about it. And, even if the most attractive buy you ever heard of comes along, don't say to yourself, "Well, I will just use this money for six months before it is needed to pay for the house and make a little profit on it." This is a very important point, and if you follow it you will be repaid for having struggled through these letters, even if you pay no attention to the rest of the suggestions.

## A Lesson from the 1929 Aftermath

4—There is a similar danger to the one last described to which I hope you may some day be subject, which will come if you have made so much money in the market that you say to yourself, "I can't possibly lose more than half of it, so it is not necessary to take half of it out of the market." In the 1929-32 bear market, I lost a good deal more than half of what I had made, and I know a number of people who lost practically everything they owned. One good friend of mine had $2 million and thought nothing could hurt him, and he now has nothing but debts and a $300 a month job.

So as to avoid misunderstanding, I do not mean that a person should never put du Pont stock in his safe deposit box as an investment. If you should be lucky enough to inherit some money, it is perfectly reasonable to treat the inheritance as a separate fund and invest it in bonds, preferred and common stocks, in accordance with the standard investment practices popular at the time. In the comments made above about an investment account, I am referring only to the stock market profits which you put away and forget.

# 14

## Dangers of Buying New Issues

YOU WILL CONSTANTLY be offered new issues of stock, sometimes of companies that are just starting business, but more often of companies that have been privately held in the past and whose owners wish to sell out.

As a general proposition, I think it is a mistake for an investor to buy a stock that hasn't been on the market for some time. A stock with a free market is at least selling at any given moment at approximately what the mass judgment of investors and speculators thinks it is worth, but when you buy a new issue you are relying on your own judgment and the underwriter's judgment, and the two of you can easily go wrong. An underwriter may, in perfect good faith, make a mistake about a company, with the result that its stock may go down shortly after the public offering. Since there are plenty of stocks available on the market, there is no point in taking this additional risk. Moreover, if you make it a definite rule not to buy new securities, you will save yourself hours of unprofitable time talking to stock salesmen.

### *Be Wary of New Stock Offerings*

There are some new issues that strike the public fancy, with the result that they are oversubscribed many times and promptly go to a premium. A stock offered at 23 might be in such demand that it would sell at 28 on the offering day. Such a circumstance does not offer a chance to make a worthwhile profit because it occurs only when everyone wants the stock. The underwriting house will then offer the stock only to its "friends", i. e., the people who do business with it regularly, or to people it wishes to line up for future business. However, every salesman in the underwriting house is anxious to please as many of his friends and prospective customers as he can, so that each one will be offered only a small number of shares.

## *Four Good Reasons to Stay Out*

If you are offered 50 shares of stock in a deal of this kind, I advise you not to take it because:

1—Your principal motive in buying the stock is not because you look upon it as a desirable speculation, but rather to get the quick profit that is presented to you practically as a gift.

2—Nine times out of ten the stock is not of a kind that you would want to keep and, accordingly, the sensible thing to do if you want to make money is to sell it out immediately.  However, if you do sell it out immediately, what was practically a gift has turned into 100% gift or a bribe to do future buisness.

3—You put yourself under obligation to the salesman or the underwriting house, so that you at least have to spend some time listening to future sales talks even if you don't fall for future offerings.

4—This kind of profit is more or less a chiseling operation which develops bad habits.

# 15

## Some "Opportunities" to Avoid

YOU ARE SURE to be offered some very wonderful opportunities in oil wells, gold mines and unique inventions. Here are some examples:

1—The X Gold Company owns 1,000 acres of gold-bearing gravel on a branch of the Sacramento River. This gravel has been tested by a prominent mining engineer and runs 50 cents a yard and there are so many thousand yards available. The figures go on to give cost of production and with a very little arithmetic you can readily see that, for every $100 put into the project, you should net at least $250 a year for the next ten years.

2—The Y Oil Company has just obtained an excellent lease that hasn't been available before because the property has been tied up in an estate and the executor has not wished to deal with any of the larger companies. Their lease lies directly between two producing wells and the Standard Oil Co. has acquired most of the surrounding property. A consulting geologist has predicted that the oil sands will be struck at six thousand feet and that a one-thousand-barrel well of 28 gravity oil is a minimum expectation. Here, again, it is perfectly evident that a $100 investment should return many thousands over a few years.

3—You may be asked to be one of a small group to promote a new process for refining oil. A pilot plant has shown that this process will do the work at one-half the cost of the best process now in use. The value of the process is furthermore attested by an experienced petroleum engineer. In addition, you notice that the group already contains some very prominent people, including the presidents of large and successful corporations. Here is a perfect chance to get in on the ground floor.

These are just examples and aren't half so good as some of the propositions that will be put up to you.

About them all, I have only one piece of advice and that is, steer clear of them. Don't even listen to anyone who wants to tell you about them because it takes up too much time and you may be tempted. I have gone into gold mines, oil wells, and inventions of all kinds and descriptions and, without exception, they have been failures. Every now and then you will hear of someone who has struck a pot of gold, but the odds against making money in this line of endeavor are very great and the chances are, if you try it here and there, you will just be frittering away small amounts and wasting much time, energy and thought on them.

## Some "Outs" You May Expect

Something always goes wrong. Either they have not made enough test holes in the gravel, or there is a fault between the adjoining oil well and your property, or salt water creeps into the well, or the invention is no good without making use of an appliance invented by some other company, etc.

Moreover, keep in mind that the engineers and inventors who promote these projects generally are receiving a block of stock for themselves or are looking for a job from the company if it can be financed, so that their opinions cannot be said to be entirely unbiased. And, lastly, never be fooled by the prominence or alleged intelligence and experience of the other people who have gone into the project—the percentage of suckers is just as high among presidents as it is among clerks when they get out of their own line of business.

## 16

## Tricks of Capitalization

THE FIRST THING TO UNDERSTAND about capitalization is the principle of leverage, which can best be explained by an example.

We will suppose that Company A has outstanding 100,000 shares of $5 dividend preferred stock and 100,000 shares of common stock, and Company B has outstanding the same 200,000 shares, but they are all common stock. Now consider the difference in earnings on the common stock if, in a good year, both companies earn $2 million and in a bad year they both earn $500,000. In the good year the preferred dividend of Company A will take $500,000, leaving $1.5 million, or $15 a share for the common, while Company B's earnings will be spread over all of the common stock and will only be $10 a share. On the other hand, in the bad year the preferred stock will take all of Company A's earnings and the common stock will earn nothing, while the common stock of Company B will earn $2.50 a share.

If we go one step further and substitute bonds instead of preferred stock in Company A's capitalization and assume that the companies earn nothing for several years, Company A is in an even worse position, because the bond interest must be paid whether it is earned or not, or the bondholders may foreclose and take over the company. This means that unless Company A had cash stored up or could borrow it somewhere (which is hard to do in a depression), the stockholders might lose everything through foreclosure of the bonds, while Company B can just stop dividends and will live through the depression and stockholders will have a chance to come back in the next rise.

Moreover, if, after the depression had been going on for two or three years, both companies saw a chance to make some money if they could raise $2 million, Company B might well be able to issue $2 million of convertible bonds and raise the money while Company A, with its

$10 million bonded indebtedness, wouldn't have a chance.

## Illusory Character of Earnings

Aside from the obvious conclusion that the companies without bonded debts are safer, the moral is to be on your guard against the illusory character of high earnings produced by monkeying with the capitalization. This overweighting of a company with senior securities with fixed returns so that all of the earnings are piled up on the common stock can be carried to such lengths that the common stock, while looking very beautiful, is nothing more than a soap bubble which will burst in the first wind. This was the case in 1929 with many railroads and with a number of holding companies, particularly in the public utility field.

You should therefore never be satisfied to find out what the earnings are on the common stock of a company without ascertaining what percentage of total earnings is available for the common stockholders. Different lines of business will show different percentages. For example, the public utility business, which up to now has been a comparatively safe one producing comparatively steady earnings, has been able to have a very much higher percentage of bonds and preferred stock than, say, a steel company which may earn $5 million one year and nothing the next.

Another time to watch for the effect of leverage is when you are buying a preferred stock for investment. The customary rule of thumb in judging the value of a bond or preferred stock is the number of times the company has earned the interest or dividend requirements. Now suppose that you have a company with $5 million of 6% bonds and $1 million of 6% preferred stock and earning $450,000. Leaving out the effect of income taxes for the sake of simplicity, the bond interest will take $300,000, which will leave $150,000 to cover the $60,000 preferred dividend, so you will hear even reasonably intelligent people saying that the company earned its preferred dividend two and one-half times. This is a most deceptive way of stating the facts, because a company can't earn a preferred dividend until it earns the prior bond interest, so that you must consider bond interest and preferred dividend requirements lumped together, and looked at in this way the company earned its bond interest plus preferred dividend only 1.20 times.

## Double Leverage of Some Holding Companies

The effect of leverage is most striking in the case of holding companies, which are companies created mainly to own the securities, mostly the common stock, of a number of other companies. You will find public utility holding companies which own the common stock of a large number of utility operating companies where both the operating companies themselves and the holding company have bonds and preferred stock outstanding. The common stock of the operating companies is subject to the leverage factor and if you take this common stock and issue bonds, preferred stock and common stock against it, there is a double leverage, with the result that the earnings on the common stock of the holding company can be wiped out with a very small decline in the total earnings of the operating companies.

One good test to apply to the common stock of a holding company is to calculate the percentage decline in the gross revenues of the operating companies which is sufficient to wipe out the income on the common stock of the holding company. Such a test may show that a superficially attractive stock has no more substance to it than the delightful aroma in a bakery shop.

It seems hardly credible, but I can remember one holding company that was formed in the twenties which owned nothing but the common stocks of three other holding companies. This fourth company also issued bonds and preferred stock, so that its common stock couldn't even be called an aroma—it was more like a whiff. Of course, what happened was that at the first sign of trouble this entire company was wiped out, bonds and preferred stock, as well as common. This is a very poignant memory, because I owned some of the bonds which I had bought because they were attractively decorated with a convertible privilege.

## Value of Participating Securities

Another trick of capitalization to look for is participating securities. It was once the fashion and may become so again for an underwriting house to take hold of a privately owned company and change its capitalization into class A stock and class B stock. We will take an instance in which the class A stock is entitled to the first $2 in dividends after which the class B stock receives $1 a share in dividends, and then all dividends are divided share for share between both classes alike.

We will suppose that there are 100,000 shares of class A offered to the public at $30 a share, that the owners of the company kept 400,000 shares of class B, and that the earnings of the company were $800,000. The class A is advertised as a participating stock combining the features of safety of a preferred stock with the chance of profit inherent in a common stock through its right to participate in the earnings, and it is pointed out that the earnings on the stock were $8 a share, i. e., $800,000 divided by 100,000 shares.

This is all perfectly true, but the trouble is that it creates an illusion that you are being offered the advantages of a common stock when you are actually being offered only a very small piece of these advantages. The statement that the earnings were $8 a share on the class A stock does show that its dividend is fairly well protected (assuming that there were no bonds outstanding which would introduce the leverage factor) but is entirely without significance when it comes to finding whether you are being offered any of the advantages of a common stock.

On all such participating stocks you must figure the earnings as though they were common stocks in order to determine how much of the advantage of a common stock they carry. In this case, the A stock is entitled to the first $200,000 of earnings and the B stock is entitled, at the rate of $1 a share, to the next $400,000 of earnings, which leaves $200,000 for the participating provision to be divided among a total of 500,000 shares of stock, or 40 cents a share. It thus appears that the earnings on the A stock, viewed as a common stock, are only $2.40 a share, so that it is by no means a bargain from that point of view at 30. While it might be a desirable investment as a preferred stock, depending upon the company and the line of business it is in, you should not be wheedled into buying it on the theory that there is much chance of profiting from the common stock feature.

A preferred stock is sometimes made to look attractive

by attaching to each share a bonus of one share of common stock. As a general proposition, I would steer clear of packages of this sort for several reasons:

### Beware of the Sweetener

1—You are interested in making money on your capital and you don't want to tie it up in preferred stock.

2—The worst kind of purchase is a weak preferred stock, as it can never go up and can easily go down, and the fact that a bonus of common is offered with the preferred shows that the preferred can't stand on its own feet.

3—You don't know just what you are paying for either stock—it is better to wait until they are split up and then buy the common if you want it.

4—If you are given a bonus of common to buy the preferred, there is a distinct possibility that the promoters are presenting themselves with an even more handsome bonus of stock as an offset.

# 17

## When to Buy Convertible Securities

A CONVERTIBLE SECURITY is a bond or preferred stock which the holder can exchange for common stock. It has the fascinating appeal of presumably carrying the safety of the bond plus the chance of profit inherent in the common stock, because if the common stock goes up, you can convert the bond into the stock and either hold the stock or sell it immediately at the available profit. In fact, you don't even have to convert, because the bond itself will go up, paralleling the rise of the common stock. There have been some very fine convertible securities, but the type is exceedingly treacherous. Here are some of the things to look for:

### *Hazards in Convertibles*

1—In the first place, it may well be that the convertible security, while called a bond, doesn't provide much more safety than a common stock. This kind of financing is often employed by companies in a weak position, and you will frequently find that when weakness appears in the common stock the anticipated security of owning the bond is no longer with you. I have seen many a convertible bond sold to the public at 100 which will stay around that price and maybe go up a few points, and then break wide open when trouble comes along. The moral is not to buy a convertible security on the theory that it gives you safety plus profit without investigating the safety factor very carefully. The mere fact that a security carries the name of "bond" or "preferred stock" is no guaranty that it will not drop just as fast as a common stock.

2—Find out, if you can, how much you are paying for the conversion privilege. You never get something for nothing, so you can be sure that when you buy a convertible bond part of the price you pay is for the conversion privilege. The ideal way is to compare the price of the convertible bond with the price of non-convertible bonds of the same company. You will often be astonished to find that, while the convertible bond looks as if it might be worth par, the other bonds are selling at, say, 88, and that you are paying perhaps 12 points for the conversion privilege.

Of course it is only rarely that you can make such a direct comparison, as the majority of companies with convertible securities will not have other bonds outstanding. However, you can usually approximate the price of the convertible privilege by comparing the price of the convertible bond with the price of the non-convertible bonds of similar companies.

## Bonds "Ex" Conversion Privilege

The investigation of how much you are paying for the conversion privilege has the additional advantage of showing you what the bond is worth without the conversion privilege and therefore giving you a pretty good test of how safe the bond is. For example, assume that grade A bonds generally are yielding 4%, that you are offered a convertible bond yielding 4%, and that you find a similar bond without the conversion privilege would sell for 88 or, counting the rise to par at maturity, would yield 6%. It is evident that the bond is by no means a grade A bond in and of itself and that in the event of a bear market you will suffer not only a loss in the bond but also the loss of a good part of the value of the conversion privilege.

As part of your investigation of what you are paying for the conversion privilege, calculate what percentage rise in the common stock is necessary before the conversion privilege can be exercised at a profit. Suppose, for example, that a bond is selling at 105 convertible into five shares of stock which is selling at 15. Or, to put it another way, that the bond is convertible into stock at 20, which means that for every point the stock rises over 20 the bond would go up five points over par. This presents, superficially at least, an attractive picture, but on a little analysis it is evident that the stock must rise 40% in value before you would gain from exercising the conversion privilege. The stock would have to go up not only to 20 but another point, in addition, because the bond is selling at 105.    Forty percent is a very handsome little profit itself and, in my opinion, it would not be worthwhile buying the bond.    If you think the stock is going up, buy the stock instead.

3—Do not buy convertible securities unless you think that the common stock of the company is an attractive medium of speculation.    There is always the temptation to say, "Well, I don't think much of a company that sells horns for automobiles, but, after all, a bond is a bond and the stock might have a speculative rise,  so I can't lose much and might profit."    The trouble with this kind of reasoning is that it entices you into second-rate companies and uses up your buying power, which could be devoted to better things, and also greatly increases your risk of loss, as you may not have carefully followed out the suggestions in paragraph 1 and bought a security which was in and of itself a good bond.

4—Convertible securities are sometimes disappointing due to being redeemed just as the common stock approaches the point where you are about to make a profit. This frequently happens, because the mere fact that the common stock is going up shows that the company is in better shape and perhaps able to finance without offering the attraction of the conversion privilege.    The moral is obviously that, between two convertible bonds of equal merit, it is better to buy the one that is not callable for a long enough period to give you a run for your money, or is callable at a sufficiently high price to assure you of a worthwhile profit if the company is a success.

5—There is a trick in convertible securities to watch for known as the graduated conversion privilege.    For example, a company will put out $5 million of bonds and will agree that the first million offered for conversion are convertible at 50, i. e., two shares of stock for each $100 of bonds, the second million convertible at 55, the third million at 60, the fourth million at 65, and the last million at 70.

## You Can't Convert for Some Time

If the stock is selling at 45, the bond will look attractive on the theory that the stock has only to go up a little over 10% before the convertible privilege begins to operate

to your profit. This is not so, however, because the
minute the stock rises slightly over 50 the first million will
be converted and the remainder won't go up. If you are
one of the first million that converts, all you have done is
buy the stock at 50 and you might as well have bought
at 45.

The bond will not reflect the advance in the price of
the stock any more than if the entire issue were convertible
at 70. There is, obviously, no sense in paying much for a
right to convert at 70 when the stock is at 45.

## Graduated Scale Arrangement

There is another kind of graduated conversion privilege that is not so bad, i. e., the company will offer the
right to convert at 50 for the first year, 55 for the second
year, etc. While this kind of privilege is, of course, not so
attractive as the right to convert at 50 throughout the life
of the bond, you nevertheless have the assurance that if the
stock does go over 50 during the first year your bond will
go up accordingly.

6—Look to see that the conversion privilege, if exercised, is not going to increase the number of common shares
outstanding to such a point as to create a large dilution of
per-share earnings and a correspondingly lesser likelihood
of the stock's going up. Dilution of earnings means
reduction of earnings per share by spreading them among
more shares. For example, suppose a company had
200,000 shares of common stock outstanding and offered
$5 million of 6% preferred convertible at 20. Now if you
anticipate that the common stock will earn $3 a share and
believe that such a stock should sell at ten times earnings
or $30 a share, you might hope for a 50% profit from the
purchase of the preferred. In order to see the true situation you must calculate what the earnings per share of
common stock would be if all the stock were converted.
In this case you assume that the company is going to
earn its preferred dividends, which would be $300,000, and
$3 per share on the common, another $600,000, or a total
of $900,000. The conversion of the preferred would
require another 250,000 shares of common stock, with the
result that there would be a total of 450,000 shares outstanding and the earnings on this stock would be only $2

a share (i. e., $900,000 divided by 450,000 shares), which would mean that at ten times earnings the stock would be worth only $20 a share and, therefore, that the conversion privilege has no immediate value.

7—Be sure that the conversion privilege is protected against split-ups, stock dividends, and offerings of rights to stockholders. Obviously, if you own a bond convertible into stock at 50 and, just as the stock approaches 50 and you start rubbing your hands, the company declares a 25% stock dividend (issuing one new share for every four shares outstanding), the stock will promptly drop to 40 and the immediate prospect of profit on your conversion privilege disappears. You can see readily that the stock would perform in this way because just increasing the number of shares outstanding doesn't make the stock as a whole more valuable and one share at 50 is the same as one and one-quarter shares at 40.

## The Option Warrants Feature

These comments concerning convertible securities apply with equal force to bonds which have option warrants attached to them entitling the holder to buy common stock at some fixed price. Moreover, there is an additional deceptive feature about option bonds to watch for. Suppose you bought a $1,000 bond that had an option to buy ten shares of common stock at 100. Then if the common stock rose 20% above the option price, you might think that the bond would also rise 20%. If it were a convertible bond it obviously would, but an option bond will not necessarily do so because, while the options could then be cashed for $200, the bond itself might not be worth par. (This defect ordinarily met in option bonds is avoided in some of them by a provision authorizing the holder to use the face amount of the bond in lieu of cash in purchasing the optioned stock).

Moreover, suppose that the option offered is to buy ten shares of stock at 20. If the stock goes up to 30, a rise of 50% over the option price, a bond convertible at 20 would likewise rise 50%. However, the option to buy ten shares would be worth only $100, which would be only a 10% profit on your bond. In order for option bonds to be at all fairly comparable to convertible bonds, they should contain an option to buy as many shares of stock at the option price as the principal amount of the bond would buy at the option price. In other words, a $1,000 bond should carry options to buy 50 shares of common stock if the option price is 20, and 20 shares if the option price is 50, and 10 shares if the option price is 100, etc.

## When to Start Shopping

The time to look for convertible bonds is when we are in a business depression which has lasted for some time and some first-class company, the stock of which you would be perfectly willing to buy if you thought we were in a bull market and which is surely going to live through any depression, offers some convertible bonds. It is probably doing so because it sees a chance to invest the money in some plant additions or improvements which it expects will make a profit—one of the first signs of the stirrings of a revival. Moreover, at the bottom of a bear market, you will probably have lost so much that you will be scared about buying anything, and this is a good way to start overcoming the fright.

# 18

## Forecasting With Statistics

*In this letter are described a number of methods
which may have value in forecasting the trends
of security prices.*

*None of them alone, the author states, is likely
to prove particularly reliable. But he does believe
that several of them, when they point in the same
direction, may serve as a valuable warning.*

*It should be noted, however, that these are
statistical methods for a peacetime economy.
The relation of production to consumption, for
instance, could hardly be measured right now,
and would be of questionable value if a measure
could be obtained. The same is true of most of the
other indexes suggested. Presumably, however,
the bases on which these indexes rest will exist again
when the war is over.—Ed.*

I APPROACH THIS SUBJECT with some misgivings
because even the people who know a good deal about it
do not appear to know enough to do them much good.
On the other hand, since the stock market reflects, or
rather endeavors to anticipate, the profits of business, it is
theoretically possible to find a set of statistics which move
enough in advance of corporate profits, or at least of our
information concerning profits, to anticipate the stock
market. In this letter I shall briefly describe a number of
forecasting methods which appear to have a sensible basis
with the thought you may be sufficiently interested to
investigate further. I hold out no hope that you will be
able to chart any single line on which you can depend,
but, if a number point the same way, they may well serve
as a valuable warning.

### Merits of the Averages

1—*Anticipatory Averages.* Possibly the oldest
form of magic line is an average of stocks which in the past

have moved ahead of the market. It is conceivable that the stocks of certain companies, because of their relationship to business as a whole or because of the knowledge of their principal stockholders who affect the market by purchases and sales, will go up or down before the market as a whole moves one way or the other. Averages of such stocks are constructed by the trial and error method, but the principal danger in such an average is that the past action of the stocks has been the result of coincidence.

The only such average that has ever influenced my own trading is an average of the motor stocks. I have noticed that Chrysler and General Motors customarily start down before the rest of the market. If they exhibit a downward trend, i.e., a break followed by a rise that fails to reach the preceding high and then a second break which carries lower than the first one, I think the market is probably going down and I sell some stocks. This may be no more sensible than a plan devised by a friend of mine for going on vacations because he found that the market went up every time he took a week off.

2—*Inventories.* When goods are piling up in inventory instead of being sold, there is danger of a general business and market decline. It is not easy to secure up-to-date, correct figures on inventories, but since many companies borrow from banks in order to carry inventories, a rise in commercial loans (the totals of which are published weekly) tends to indicate increased inventories and a decline to indicate a reduction in inventories. However, as business becomes more active, there is more need for inventories, since a company selling 100 articles a month obviously must have more on hand and in the process of manufacture than when it is only selling 50. Accordingly, changes in commercial loans or inventories which are not compared to public demand would not have the significance you were looking for and, therefore, you must have a ratio between demand and inventories.

Demand can be represented by bank debits, i.e., the amount of checks drawn. It is customary to exclude New York city debits because the financing transactions reflected in the New York figures tend to make them less accurate indexes of commercial demand. If you compare these two sets of figures and find that the ratio of bank debits to commercial loans is going up, then inventories are probably not rising so fast as demand, which is a good sign, while if the ratio is going down, inventories are probably increasing in relation to demand, which is a bad sign. This index worked well in predicting the 1937 decline, and in predicting the bottom in 1938 by turning sharply upward.

## When the Two Lines Cross—

3—*Relation of Production to Consumption.* Another way of reaching the same result is to chart an index of consumption for several years past from some such figures as weekly department store sales and chart on transparent paper a weekly index of production for the same period. The production line is placed below the consumption line and then shoved up so that the peaks of the production line protrude through the consumption line. If the chart is any good, these peaks should come before declines in business.

The whole trick lies in selecting the right indexes; otherwise, the two lines will cross each other with no more relation to the stock market than sheep trails on a hillside. Two such charts I have run across, each prepared with different indexes, predicted the 1929 and 1937 drops. Or perhaps it would be more accurate to say they would have predicted these drops if they had been born sooner, because I believe they were constructed by selecting the indexes after the event. The inventors are carrying forward the same figures from week to week and consider it a reasonable expectation that the lines will cross again before the next big decline.

Incidentally, I wouldn't pay any attention to a chart made up by a man who wants to keep his indexes a secret any more than you would take a patent medicine without knowing its contents.

## New Orders as a Forecaster

4—*New Orders.* Companies obviously must get orders in advance of their sales, so that if you could find a proper index of new orders, you would have a pretty good idea of how business is going for the near future. There are a number of indexes of new orders, but so far none of them that I have seen appears to have any particular value in forecasting business changes. However, statisticians are constantly working on ways of compiling an index of new orders, and this is a development that seems to me worth watching.

## Sensitiveness of Commodity Prices

5—*Commodity Prices.* As a general proposition, an upward trend in commodity prices is good for business and a downward trend is bad. An ordinary index of commodity prices has little forecasting value because, by the time it has made a marked move, business and the market will have already taken this move into account. However, certain commodities move faster than others and are more sensitive to changes. If you could pick an index of a few commodities which generally change in price before the great body of commodities changes, you would obviously have a valuable indication of a coming trend. For instance, *Barron's* publishes an index of sensitive spot commodity prices and another index of commodity futures prices. Both these indexes had established a clear downward trend by the middle of August, 1937, before the market broke badly.

## Anticipating Profit Margins

6—*Profit Margins.* The trend of profit margins, i.e., the difference between the selling price and cost of production, is an obvious indication of business prosperity or depression. If you wait until the companies' annual reports are issued, it will be too late, because the market will usually have gone up or down enough to take into account the facts as disclosed by the reports. Here, again, it is possible to prepare an index of prices received and an index of production costs which should indicate with some degree of accuracy what the reports are going to show when they come out.

By using the same method of shoving the production cost line (drawn on transparent paper) up to where its peaks cross the selling price line, one such index I have seen was constructed so that these protruding peaks came just before the market declines in 1929 and 1937, and if the figures are carried forward, they might predict future declines.

## *Sources of Data*

The figures needed for these indexes can be culled out of available publications, but the best thing to do is to induce your broker to hire someone to prepare the material in usable form or subscribe to some publication or economic service which publishes them regularly.

## 19

## Don'ts on Receiving Advice and Information

RELIABLE INFORMATION ON the earnings and prospects of a company is, of course, extremely valuable and likewise extremely hard to get. Possibly I should say that the hardest part is not to get the information, but to tell whether it is reliable, because many people will, in perfectly good faith, give you information which is erroneous for one reason or another. You will have to use your own judgment on the reliability. Here are a few general don'ts:

(a) Don't take information from customers' men in brokerage houses unless they will put it in writing and tell you the source. Much of it is pure gossip, and you have no way of knowing when they happen to be right.

(b) Don't gossip with acquaintances about the market and act on what they tell you. If information is volunteered, always check it very carefully. People like to show off their knowledge and very often if they haven't the knowledge they do the showing off anyway. I don't mean that they will be deliberately dishonest, but that they will unconsciously attach weight to rumors and magnify estimates merely for the purpose of having something to say to which others will listen.

(c) Be wary of information from anyone connected with an underwriting house. It is very likely to concern stock they have underwritten or are about to underwrite and which they want to go up. Consequently, their information tends to be colored with their natural enthusiasm for conducting a successful operation.

For example, a salesman once told me the earnings on a certain stock were running at the rate of $6 a share. I asked him how he knew and he replied that he had heard the news from a partner in his firm, a director of the company, who had just received the latest monthly report. As it happened I, too, knew a director who had just received a monthly report. On inquiry, he verified the statement that the report showed 50 cents a share earned for the last month, but added that it had been an exceptional month, that the monthly directors' reports do not contain any provision for income taxes and depreciation, and that with all these factors considered, the annual earnings were actually running at the rate of about $3 a share.

(d) Don't take tips from anyone. By a tip I mean a suggestion to purchase a security, unaccompanied by information as to why it is a good buy. By anyone, I include even the presidents of the companies. If the president will tell you about his company's earnings, you can use your own judgment as to whether or not it is a good buy, but the mere fact that a man is very good at running his business doesn't mean that he knows anything about the market.

(e) Investigate carefully before subscribing to a general supervising investment counsel service which tells you when to buy and sell. They have so much money to manage that it is difficult for them to do a really good job for a casual subscriber. The fundamental difficulty with these large firms, even if they are acting in the highest good faith, which as far as I know they all do, is that they handle so much money they can't move fast enough and often hesitate to move at all for fear that their buying or selling will affect the market too much.

Furthermore, their size prevents them from having anything to do with stocks that do not have the broadest possible market. While such a market is very desirable for anyone, there are obviously stocks with enough market to suit an individual trading in a few hundred shares which would be impossible trading media for an investment counsel firm or trust that deals only in many thousands of shares.

(f) Don't make a deal with anyone to give him a percentage of the profits if you accept his advice. There is too much temptation on him to put you into the riskiest type of security on the chance that it will produce a large profit and, therefore, a large percentage.

# 20

## Where and How to Get Information—A Parting Admonition

COMING NOW TO DESIRABLE ways of getting information, first comes your reading. You should subscribe to *Barron's* and read it from cover to cover every week. It will give you an invaluable background of general knowledge about stocks, keep you in touch with current developments on inventions and new processes, and will frequently serve the purpose of calling your attention to stocks which, on further study, appear to be good purchases.

Secondly, I strongly recommend your making as many contacts as possible with professional investment counselors who are willing to take the job, not of managing your account, but of giving you reports from time to time on companies that they consider desirable. There are two men I know of now who occasionally bring me information about companies they have studied carefully and, if the stock appeals to me and I buy it, I pay them a percentage of the investment. These men can sometimes secure very close contacts with the companies in which they are interested and will be able to give you information on trends and coming developments that you cannot secure from any publication. Never hesitate to pay such a man a good fee because, no matter what he charges, it will be very small compared to the potential gain or loss from acting on the information he provides.

Thirdly, do not hesitate to write the president of a company that you are considering the purchase of some of the company's stock and ask him for the information you want. This direct method is usually ignored because no one thinks it will work, but you will be surprised at how often you will run into a man who is willing to be entirely frank. It helps if you buy five or ten shares of the stock and have it registered in your name before you write.

Fourth, do business with a broker who appeals to you personally and who has customers with important posi-

tions in the community. He will occasionally be author-
ized by some of his other customers to pass on valuable
items of news about their companies.

Lastly come your friends. If you know someone in
a company, he is generally delighted to tell you anything
you want to know about it.

## Brokerage Literature and Miscellany

Of course, before receiving any information you
should educate yourself as much as possible so that you
will know how to understand and interpret it. For this
purpose I recommend that you read all the text books
you can get on the analysis of securities, and also read as
many reports on securities as you can. Brokerage houses
are constantly putting out reports on this or that company
in order to encourage their customers to buy, and the
more of these you read the easier it will be to make practical application of the information you receive. I don't
mean for you to follow the advice in these reports, at least
until you have had enough training so that you can tell
which are good and which are bad, but you want to try to
get as much practice as possible in judging the value of
securities from a given set of facts

One final word of warning about information—always
remember that you must decide things for yourself. You
will, of course, never give anyone the discretionary right
to buy and sell stocks in your account, but if you do too
much talking with other people you are giving them a
partial discretion by allowing them to confuse your mind,
if not influence it. You can't help being influenced by
other people's opinions, so don't talk to people just to
"get their ideas." If you expose yourself to too many
points of view, you will find yourself losing the power to
make up your own mind and the decisiveness which are so
essential.

In this connection there is one type of free information
to which you cannot avoid being subjected but which
should be completely ignored. I refer to public statements
of reassurance emitted by prominent figures whenever
there is a panic in the market. For example, the head of a
large automobile company will announce: "Our business
has never been better and we are looking forward to a fine

year.  Fundamental conditions are sound and there is no
cause for alarm."  Whenever you read such a statement—
or, for that matter, any prediction on the market—it is not
a bad idea to ask yourself whether you can imagine the
same individual expressing a contrary view.  You would
doubt your senses if you heard such a man say: "I believe
we are on the verge of a serious depression in which the
automobile business will suffer with all others.  If we sell
half as many cars next year as we have sold this year we
will be lucky."

If you cannot expect a man ever to make a pessimistic
statement, what value can you attach to his optimistic
remarks?  His optimism is not necessarily false, but the
mere fact that his company manufactures a good product
does not in and of itself qualify him as a seer on business
conditions or the stock market.  Since both the success
of his company and his personal success are bound up with
the feeling of well being on the part of the public which
induces the purchase of automobiles, refrigerators, houses,
etc., it is unreasonable to expect him to avoid the bias
which classifies his expressions as the result of wishful
thinking or as a sort of coach's pep talk to a losing team.

I cannot possibly overemphasize the importance of
relying entirely on your own judgment.  If you depend
upon others to settle the question of bull or bear market
or what stocks to buy, you will never have any confidence
in what you are doing; you will be worried by conflicting
opinions and you will never stick to one course of action
long enough to make any money.  Advice is bound to be
about evenly divided because the market price of a stock
at any given moment represents the composite judgment
of its value of everyone interested in it.  If you make up
your mind that a stock is a good buy and know why you
have done so, then when your broker tells you that the
best stock market service in the country predicts the stock
will slump, say, 50%, you can calmly tell him his service
is crazy and go your own way.  When you let others make
your decision for you, you are no longer engaged in stock
trading, but in a guessing game as to which piece of advice
is right; in other words, you are a gambler and not a speculator, and you had better quit.

# 21

## Why Giving Advice Is Bad

THE SUBJECT OF GIVING advice could be disposed of in one short sentence—don't do it.

There are two kinds of situations in which one gives advice on the market; formally taking on the job of advising someone concerning his or her investments. and casual advice given to friends to the effect that such-and-such a stock looks good or that you have recently bought some shares of a given company. So far as formal advice is concerned, you should do your best to avoid accepting any responsibility about anyone else's investments, even members of your family.

The job of advising someone on investments is a regular professional job, just as difficult, if not more so, as being a doctor or a lawyer, and should be left entirely to professionals in the business. Of course you can't sit by and say nothing while your sister is throwing away her money, but it is much better to make her consult an alleged expert than to tell her what to do yourself.

Casual advice and information to friends are not quite so bad, but can have unfortunate results. For example, if you tell a friend that you are informed that such-and-such a company is going to earn $2 a share during the current quarter and that you have bought some of the stock, and then find out that the information is incorrect what do you do? Of course you must telephone him and tell him, but if you don't know whether or not he has bought any of the stock, you feel pretty silly in doing so and, even if you did know that he bought some of the stock, you may have forgotten that you gave him the information or he may be out of town when you sell your stock.

If you acquire the habit of benevolently giving forth any facts that may come to your attention, you can't possibly keep track of all the people you have talked to, and yet you are bound to feel yourself somewhat responsible if they buy the stock and perhaps take a loss on it through not getting out in time when you have taken a profit.

The best way to avoid giving advice or information is never to let anyone know that you consider yourself capable of doing so, and then you won't be asked. Information of this kind is like strong drink—you should give it only to people you are sure can handle it. But to these you should give it freely if for no other reason than that you are more likely to get some in return.

# 22

### You Don't Have to Make Money

"YOU DON'T have to make money in the market"—
or at least if you do, you had better keep away from
it. Nail this idea into your minds, because it is the most
important advice on the subject you'll ever get from me
or anyone else.

If you can't keep yourself in this frame of mind, your
chance of success is just about hopeless, and not only
will you lose your money but you'll also ruin your happi-
ness and you'll make a failure of your job. Remember
that your job is your main source and your only reliable
source of income and support, so it is foolish to jeopardize
its success for the sake of a pure possibility, however
entrancing. It is quite a risk to encourage anyone to deal
in the market, but I am taking the risk in the hope that
you boys will have enough strength of character to drop
it absolutely if you find that you can't treat it as a side
line and that it is affecting your attention to your main
job in life.

The stock market can be pure poison to a man and
one test of whether the poison has entered into you is
whether you are using market profits to pay your living
expenses. It is all right to take money out of the market
to buy a house or to take a trip you wouldn't otherwise
take, but never, under any circumstances, let yourself
fall into the trap of adopting a standard of living that is
dependent to the slightest extent on stock market profits.

As a corollary to this advice, whenever the market
bothers you so that you think about it at the office or worry
about it at night after you go to bed, sell down to the
point where you regain your detached attitude, or, as it
is sometimes put, "Sell down to the sleeping point." The
market will always be there waiting for you to come back
when you want to.

### Need Not Own Stocks All the Time

Also, whenever a broker urges you to buy a stock

and you don't feel confident he is right, say over to yourself, "I don't have to make money in the market," and do nothing. Don't hesitate to keep your money in cash for a year or more if you have no firm conviction. You don't have to play every spin of the wheel. The market is a never-ending game of "Red Dog", where you can sit back and bet only when you are convinced the odds are way in your favor and, furthermore, the only ante you have to pay while you are waiting is loss of interest on your cash, which is trivial compared to the stakes you are playing for. Four percent on $25,000 is only $1,000 a year, which is ten points on 100 shares of stock.

If, while you are waiting, the market has a big rise or fall from which you have not profited, don't let it worry you. You still have your money, which is all you would have if you had never known anything about the market. What you make on the market is just extra. Brokers may tell you that you are losing an opportunity. This is just about as sensible as to say you have lost an opportunity when you fail to bet on number 7 if that is the number that turns up. It isn't an opportunity for you unless you are convinced of what you want to do. The biggest urging you will have to combat in following this idea is this urging from brokers. Naturally they can't make money out of commissions if their customers are doing nothing, so that they unconsciously acquire an attitude of mind that if you don't buy you should sell, and they completely overlook the third alternative of doing nothing.

Always remember—"You don't have to make money in the market."